So You Want to Lead Students

So You Want to Lead Students

CHUCK KLEIN

Tyndale House
Publishers, Inc.
Wheaton, Illinois

First Printing, July 1982

Library of Congress Catalog Card Number 80-50904
ISBN 0-8423-6084-0, paper

Printed in the United States of America

CONTENTS

Preface **What's This Book All About?** 7

How to Use **SO YOU WANT TO LEAD STUDENTS** 9

SECTION ONE—**Teaching and Leading Students**

Introduction **So You Want to Lead Students** 13

One **Understanding the Culture in Which We Work** 17

Two **How Learning Takes Place** 21

Three **An Environment for Learning and Growing** 25

Four **Getting Your Group Together** 31

Five **How to Plan for Your Meeting—Teaching That Gets Results** 37

Six **A Sample Lesson Plan** 45

Seven **Putting Together the Loose Pieces** 49

SECTION TWO—**How to Use the SO YOU Books**

One **How to Use SO YOU WANT SOLUTIONS—Chapter by Chapter** 55

Two **How to Use SO YOU WANT TO GET INTO THE RACE—Chapter by Chapter** 75

Three **How to Use SO YOU WANT TO SET THE PACE—Chapter by Chapter** 93

PREFACE:
WHAT'S THIS BOOK ALL ABOUT?

So You Want to Lead Students is a book designed specifically to help you in your effectiveness with students. How will it help?

1. It will give you insight into our contemporary culture, and how the student is affected by the dynamics of this culture.
2. It will give you insight into how a student learns, and how he perceives and applies truth to his life.
3. It will give a plan for teaching—a plan that will win.
4. It will give you insight into how to use and teach each of the books in the *So You* series:
   So You Want Solutions
   So You Want to Get into the Race
   So You Want to Set the Pace

Investing your life in others, helping them to grow up in Christ, is one of the richest experiences of the entire Christian life. We want your experience to be especially gratifying and fruitful. That's the motivation behind this book. It's your tool and you are the craftsman. A good craftsman is creative in how he uses his tools.

HOW TO USE SO YOU WANT TO LEAD STUDENTS

So You Want to Lead Students is divided into two sections. Section One gives insight into working with today's student, as well as principles and how to's for effective teaching. Section Two then takes a chapter-by-chapter look at each of the three books in the *So You* series, giving insights into how to teach each chapter.

Some of the principles for teaching included in this book were popularized in the seventies by Gospel Light's International Center for Learning. For additional study I highly recommend that you obtain a copy of *Ways to Help Them Learn,* as well as a copy of *Bible Learning Activities for Youth.* Both are published by Gospel Light Publications, Ventura, CA 93006.

Several principles taught in this book have also been adapted from *Game Plan* written by Diana McGinty and Chuck Klein and published by Campus Crusade for Christ, San Bernardino, CA 92414.

Leading and Teaching Students

INTRODUCTION
SO YOU WANT TO LEAD STUDENTS

After thinking for a moment, the seventeen-year-old candidly responded, "I believe in God . . . if there is one." In his own uncanny way the young man provided a vivid analysis of today's youth culture—a generation that wants to find a reason to believe, but usually ends up overwhelmed with doubt.

This is the student generation today. They are the product of everything that our society has worked so hard to produce over the last several decades: negativism, no system of absolutes, and—most destructive—a humanistic philosophy that deceives people into believing they can solve their own problems—without God.

Our culture is draining young people of the very substance for living. With the exception of a few materialistic goals, we have left them with little to believe in, little to get excited about. It is not hard to understand why so many students appear passive and unmotivated, selfishly wrapped up in themselves. Self-gratification continues to be status quo. It is also not difficult to understand why the use of alcohol among students continues to rise. Nearly 4 million teenagers in America are problem drinkers. Perhaps we can also see a little more clearly why, tragically, the suicide rate among teenagers has tripled in recent years.

These are the symptoms of a youth culture with too little to believe in, too little to live for—a culture alienated from the God who created them. Where is this generation heading? What is their destiny? *The answer lies totally with those who will lead them—who will get involved in their culture.*

And students are looking for someone who will lead them, someone who will give them direction. In a recent survey, George Gallup showed that the vast majority of teenagers would welcome the same strength of values as their elders. They want a greater emphasis on family, hard work and authority. The overwhelming majority feel that discipline is not strong enough, and that schoolwork is too easy.

Students are simply expressing a very strong felt need. By and large, kids are not getting direction. They are not challenged. To a large extent the parental generation of our culture is still living in its own state of adolescent paralysis. Parents are preoccupied with "adult toys," obsessed with making money, terrified by the economy (no more adult toys), devoid of meaningful values and priorities, and in many cases, all too passive in rearing their own children.

Where does this leave our young people? The result is an intense frustration . . . a hunger for answers. Their spirits cry out. Those who keep a keen eye on today's young people know that students are spiritually restless and want a strong religious faith. The problem, however, is that many young people find organized religion today to be spiritually lifeless. So what do they do? To feel fulfilled, they are flirting with a wide variety of movements including transactional analysis, Zen, psychosynthesis, est, biofeedback, groping, sensitivity sessions, pyramid power, pendulum power, color psychology, astrology, tarot cards, organic food, biorhythms.[1] Young people want solutions. Why are we letting them settle for counterfeits?

In these last years of the twentieth century, we face an immense challenge—reaching the first generation of America's post-Christian era. In Mark 16:15, Jesus tells us, "*Go into all the world and preach the Good News. . . .*" Are you ready to take hold and heed the call? Students are not concerned with your ability or your training. They want to know if you care about them. Are you willing to get involved in their lives? Are you willing to take the lead, to use tough love, to give the direction they are dying for? The results of the Gallup youth surveys give us a clear directive. It behooves the churches of America to devise a whole new set of *creative ministries* to make use of young people's desire to serve and their need to believe.

Creative ministries are the result of planning by men and women with vision, leaders whose hearts are controlled by the Lord Jesus Christ. So what do you say? Are you ready to dig in? You have only one life to live. Let's get started.

NOTES

1. Gallup Youth Survey as quoted in *Seventeen* Magazine, November, 1980, page 137.

ONE
UNDERSTANDING THE CULTURE IN WHICH WE WORK

A great need that faces young Christians, and those who lead these young Christians, is biblical material that communicates within their particular culture. In other words, we need material that takes into account the learning habits of our generation. Material that does this is what we will call *culturalized* material. To *culturalize* means to design a book or tool with an understanding of the uniquenesses of a particular audience. It takes into account their learning habits, their attention span, their ability to visualize what is being taught, and their ability to apply truth.

We live in what is called the "sight and sound" generation. This unique visual and sound orientation has been an integral part of our culture since the sixties. It's a phenomenon that is probably here to stay. What exactly is the sight and sound generation? Here are some characteristics:

A short attention span. People in our day who are able to sit and listen or read for a long period of time are rare. This is not a generation of readers—tragic, but true. The reasons—the jam-packed pace of our society, the anxiety of our times, and, of course, television. The length of programming between television commercials is the average attention span of many young people today.

Second, *this generation learns more by seeing than by reading or hearing.* Why? It is called the vid-kid generation—"vid" being short for video (television). We have been conditioned to learn by seeing a picture, rather than by visualizing a picture in our minds.

I remember that when I was a child, my mother would sit with us and read stories—with no pictures. We would visualize the story in our minds. It stimulated creativity, imagination, and good learning habits. But today's studies show that the more a child watches television, the less creative he is, the slower he learns, and the less excited he is about life. It's a problem that has affected all of us to some degree. So, if we are going to communicate in today's culture we have to meet people where they are.

Third, *this generation is conditioned to handle truth as an option, not an absolute.* "Hey," says the typical relativistic student who is a product of our academic system, "if you want to believe in Jesus as God, that's fine for you, but I'm not into that." What he *is* into is handling the concept of truth as something optional, something obsolete. He's into synthesis—measuring truth totally against his own experience. "How can you know the truth? No one knows for sure! There is no real truth and I'm not responsible to anyone."

He hit it squarely on the head—*responsibility.* Who wants to be responsible if he can find a way out?

This thinking has infected all of us to some degree. As Christians we have learned to give intellectual assent to truth, but in reality we don't believe it, otherwise we would do something about it. Relativistic thinking is not a new problem. James said 1900 years ago, "Remember, it is a message to obey, not just to listen to" (James 1:22).

Part of the problem with relativism in the body of Christ has been caused by us—the Christian leaders. For too many years we have sat around and encouraged Christian kids to "rap" or "build relationships," but never challenged them to commit themselves to the truth, never given them tracks to run on. We have treated the teaching of biblical truth much too passively. Only the truth of God's Word, administered by the Holy Spirit, renews minds and changes lives.

Frankly speaking, students at the end of the twentieth century are dying for someone who will help them establish some absolutes, handles to grab onto. Our ministry style and our materials need to provide these handles—opportunities for thinking, for application, and for commitment.

Now, if this is the generation we are working with, just how will the *So You* series help in your communication?

1. The studies are designed artistically and graphically to work within a student's short attention span.
2. The studies are illustrated to help the student visualize the truth being taught.
3. The studies deal with the issues that contemporary

growing Christians need and want to understand.

4. The spiritual content is communicated clearly and precisely, yet simply.
5. Questions in each study are designed to help the student discover truth for himself. Thus he owns the knowledge, and he is more motivated to do something about it.
6. Application and learning projects in the studies provide the process through which a student must travel if he is going to learn. Telling and listening do not equal learning. Learning takes place when truth is applied.

This leader's guide is designed to help you communicate God's truth in today's contemporary culture. We have talked about our culture. Let's now take a look at how learning actually takes place.

TWO
HOW LEARNING TAKES PLACE

As we said earlier, teaching is not telling, and learning is not listening. In the early seventies David A. Stoop and Gospel Light's International Center for Learning (ICL) popularized some very basic but profound principles for teaching and learning. Simply stated *learning is what the learner does, not what the teacher does.*[1] The teacher's responsibility is to provide an *environment* where learning can take place.

There are two basic styles of teaching. The first is what we might call the *teacher-centered* style. This method involves the teacher who is equipped to the hilt with information for his students. The typical meeting or study time focuses primarily on one person—the teacher. He's excited by all the information *he* has acquired in preparing for the lesson. The students, however, are moderately to desperately bored. They are being *told* the information. To learn, they must also discover truth for themselves.

The second style of teaching is called the *learner-centered* method. This method involves telling but it goes far beyond that. Learner-centered teaching gives the student an opportunity to take the information being taught and apply it within his own life style and experience. He discovers truth as he applies it to his life.

We all learn best when we use the greatest number of our senses in the learning process. The results from studies done at the Industrial Education Department, University of Texas, show that our generation remembers:[2]

10 percent of what we read (e.g., a book).
20 percent of what we hear (a speaker).
30 percent of what we see (a poster—billboard).
50 percent of what we hear and see (a TV program).
70 percent of what we say (when we give a talk).
90 percent of what we say and do (when we talk and get involved in the action).

It is obvious that the more senses we use in learning, the more we are going to remember facts and apply them to our lives. In fact, if we rely only on reading and hearing, our students are going to remember very little, and what they do remember they may not even understand. However, you will notice that the senses of sight and personal involvement bring retention almost to a maximum.

So how can we be satisfied if we are teachers who *only tell* the facts? We simply have not taught until we have provided opportunities for our learners to personalize and apply the biblical facts being taught. Teaching involves:

1. Communicating facts.
2. Helping learners translate the facts into their life and experience.
3. Encouraging learners to apply the facts to their lives *that week.*

As I stated earlier, the books in the *So You* series are tools to help you freshly and creatively communicate biblical facts and provide tracks for challenge and application. Your job is to use these tools creatively and help the student apply the facts of the lesson to his daily life. We will discover that this is accomplished through proper preparation on your part and the use of learning and application activities.

NOTES

1. David A. Stoop, *Ways to Help Them Learn (Youth-Grades 7-12)* (Ventura, CA. Gospel Light Publications, 1971) p. 33.
2. Diana McGinty, *Game Plan* (San Bernardino, CA: Campus Crusade for Christ) p. 12.

THREE
AN ENVIRONMENT FOR LEARNING AND GROWING

In our humanistic-oriented society it has become popular to credit a person's condition to his environment. "He's a product of his environment"; so goes the familiar saying. Obviously, this philosophy, if taken to its purest extreme, would mean that all of man's problems are caused by something outside of himself, not from something within. However, if we know anything of God's Word we know this is not true. Jesus said, "For from within, out of men's hearts, come evil thoughts of lust, theft, murder, adultery, . . ." (Mark 7:21).

But it is true that one's environment can *encourage* the nature that is within him. One who lives in a lawless environment, for example, may be a likely candidate to grow up to be a lawless person. Check with your local prison inmates.

This principle is true for the opposite side of the coin also. When someone becomes a Christian, he becomes a new creation (2 Corinthians 5:17). God gives him a new nature and he gives the person his Holy Spirit to help him grow as a new creation in Christ. Our responsibility as spiritual leaders is to *provide an environment* wherein the Holy Spirit is free to work in a young Christian's life. This is the key to the learning process. This is where spiritual growth takes place.

How do you *build* an environment in which the Holy Spirit can work and growth can take place? Here are the ingredients.

1. *Your faith—your walk with the Lord.* Your environment begins with you. It begins as you demonstrate to your learners that you are placing your confidence in the sovereignty of God. Not only does this release God's power in your life, but it gives your learning environment a very positive and exciting atmosphere. Students are imitators and you are demonstrating the very basis of the Christian walk. You are demonstrating faith.

2. The second ingredient is *your personal relationship with your learners.* Ask yourself these simple questions. How well do you know your students? Are you personal friends with them, or are you an impersonal teacher who shows up once a week to impart the truth?

Relationships are the *avenue of influence.* You can pretty much count on your ministry being as effective as your relationships. I wonder how effective Jesus would have been had he not personalized his relationship with his disciples. I wonder how long his disciples would have endured had they not had the memories of their personal interaction with their Lord. Relationships open the doors to learning and commitment, not to you, but through you to Jesus Christ. It has been said *if they love you, they will love your message.* (For practical insights on how to build relationships with your learners, no matter how many years may separate you, see chapter eight of *So You Want to Set the Pace.*)

3. The third ingredient for your environment is your *program.* Most of us would put activities and program as number one in our environment. They are not. They are right where they should be—number three. The reason most programs and activities do not work is that the first two ingredients of our environment are weak or nonexistent.

Each individual activity in your program should be a special environment where students can either be introduced to Christ or grow in their relationship with Christ. All of your activities together form the total program of your environment for spiritual growth. Let's take a look.

The activities within your ministry environment should include five levels or opportunities for growth and commitment.[1] As your church or campus ministry grows you should have activities available at all levels. That way every student will have a place to be challenged, depending on his maturity and motivation.

Each level requires a little more commitment—a greater challenge. Once a person completes a study group at Level Three, for example, he can be challenged to receive more training at Level Four. However, your responsibility is to present the opportunity to him,

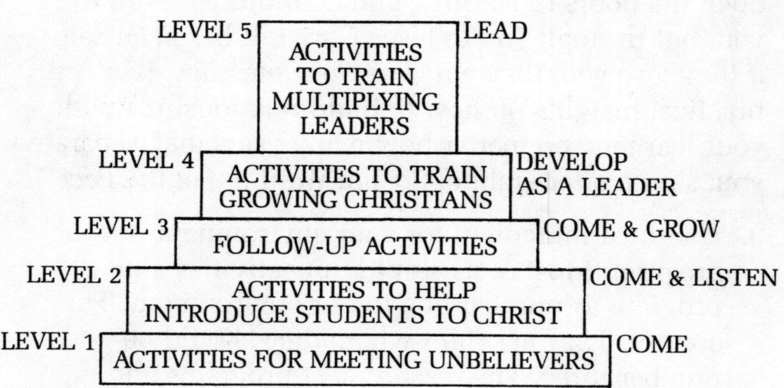

challenge him to respond, but then let the Holy Spirit work in his life. The Holy Spirit will use the example of your *faith,* the love of your *relationship* with the learner and the opportunity and the challenge within the *program.* You see, you have provided *all* the ingredients to allow the Holy Spirit the freedom to work. You don't have to twist the student's arm. Relax. You can trust the Lord for the results.

So what are we saying? The Holy Spirit is the one who is ultimately responsible for your ministry. His work in the lives of your learners includes three areas. First, he provides the *inner motivation* that our learners need if they are going to grow up in Christ (Philippians 4:13). Second, he helps the learner to *understand the meaning of God's Word* (John 14:26). And third, the Holy Spirit helps the learner *understand how to apply God's Word to his life.*

So the Holy Spirit gives *motivation, understanding,* and *willingness to apply.* This is why Paul said in Philippians 2:13, "For God is at work within you, helping you want to obey him, and then helping you do what he wants."

Our task is to provide the environment in which he can work. The *So You* books are designed as study material for third- fourth- and fifth-level activities. *So You Want Solutions* can also be used at Level Two.

NOTES
1. For more insight into your ministry environment, see *A Guidebook to Discipleship*, Harvest House Publishers, Eugene, Oregon.

FOUR
GETTING YOUR GROUP TOGETHER

The *So You* books can be used in any size group or activity within your ministry environment—campus Bible studies, Sunday school, youth group meetings, small discipleship groups, and one-on-one. As we said, each of these groups is a special environment within your larger environment for learning and growing. The *So You* books are designed to communicate biblical facts in a creative way. Your job is to maintain the environment and help your learners take the personal responsibility to apply these facts to their daily lives.

If you are beginning with some new students who have not yet been gathered together (in other words, it is not a Sunday school class, youth group, etc.), here are some guidelines for gathering your group. These guidelines are best suited for gathering smaller discipleship groups.

1. *Pray* before you do anything else. Take time to talk with God, asking him to direct you to the people whom he wants in your group. Our responsibility is to seek him for his direction.

2. *Make a list* of people you think would be good candidates for your group. As you consider who might be on your list, take into account these factors:
   a) What are the spiritual needs of this person? You might list some of the needs you think this person has.
   b) Is this a person who wants to grow in his or her relationship with Jesus Christ?
   c) Is this person one who would likely make him- or herself available to meet with you and be part of a discipleship group?

When Paul instructed Timothy in 2 Timothy 2:2 to find men for his discipleship group, he asked him to find men who were *faithful* and *able*. A faithful person is one who is *willing to apply* what he is taught. An able person is one who is of such *character* that he is able and willing to communicate what he is learning to others. To be *able* does not mean that one has to have great talent. Rather, Paul is talking in 2 Timothy 2:2 about the character of an individual. Young Christians, of course, are not going to show a great amount of spiritual character. But you will be able to tell whether or not they are willing to learn and apply. If they are, they are good candidates for your group.

3. After you have made your list, pray and ask God to give each one of these individuals a desire to grow in their relationship with him. Then *contact each one* personally and tell him of your desire to grow

spiritually and to help him grow also. Explain that you are beginning a discipleship group and you would like him to consider being a member.

Ask each one the following questions.

a) What special needs do you feel you have right now as a Christian?
b) In what areas do you desire to grow in your relationship with Christ?
c) To help with your spiritual growth will you commit yourself to attend a weekly meeting that will be ______ minutes long for ______ weeks?
d) To be in this discipleship group you will need to buy a study manual. Are you willing and able to buy a manual?
e) Are you willing to do your assignments each week and come prepared to the meetings?

4. Before you challenge each student to become part of your group, decide on two or three different *times* during the week that you can have your discipleship meeting. Give these times to each student you meet with and ask him which time would be best for him. Go with the best time for all.

   Explain that in addition to the scheduled meetings, you want to spend personal time with each individual having fun and interacting on a very personal level.

5. Give each of the students three days to a week to decide on their environment. Get back in touch with him and *ask for his decision.*

   These then, are the five steps to gathering your group. *Prayer, list of people, individual challenge, time choice,* and get *a decision.*

You are probably wondering what to do when there are large numbers of students in your church or organization who need to be followed up and discipled. If this is your situation, it is best to recruit several other leaders whom you can train to lead and disciple students. Give them the same directions you have received in this book. As you train more and more students, many of them will also be able to lead other students. You soon will have a multiplication network. This is what New Testament Christianity is all about.

WHEN YOU MEET

What are some ideas for conducting your group meeting? Let's take a look. A good length for your meeting is forty to fifty minutes. The meeting has to *keep moving*. Remember, students have a short attention span.

1. Decide on a *regular time and place* to meet. This is very important. It helps to create stability in your group. The place should be quiet, well lighted, comfortable, and suited to the size of your group. (Don't put a small group in a large room, etc.)
2. Begin your meeting with an *interaction and sharing time*.

   Have a couple of questions ready that will inspire feedback. Questions can relate to their week, their last study, etc. If you know of someone in the group who has had an interesting experience ask him or her to share it with the others. Take five to ten minutes to open your group.

3. After your sharing time take a few minutes to *talk to the Lord*. Ask him to help each member understand the facts of the study you are about to discuss. Have students lead this prayer.

4. *Teach and discuss* the study. (We will take a good look at this in the section *How to Plan for Your Group Meeting.*)
5. End your meeting with *conversational prayer.* This gives the students an opportunity to think, pray for one another, and ask for God's direction in applying the facts of the study.
6. *Plan for the week.* Take time to discuss ministry activities that your group will be involved in that week. These activities include outreach, personal appointments with your students, etc.

FIVE
HOW TO PLAN FOR YOUR MEETING

In the Greek language, Paul used two words to explain and describe knowledge. One referred to intellectual knowledge—*head knowledge*. The other referred to experiential knowledge—*heart knowledge*.

When Paul encouraged Christians to *grow in the grace and knowledge of our Lord Jesus Christ*, the word he most often used was the one for experiential knowledge. In other words, Paul wanted Christians to grow by experiencing the person of Jesus Christ in their lives—his presence, peace, and power. Paul wasn't interested only in how much his Christian friends knew intellectually. He wanted to know if they were applying the truth to their lives and were actually being changed as a result.

That is exactly the focus we are to have in our ministries. Are our students growing and changing? Is their life style, their behavior, their attitude a little different because of the truth we are teaching? These are the questions we must ask ourselves.

IT BEGINS WITH YOU!

If learning is applying facts, then how can we provide opportunities for our students to learn? Perhaps the first question you must ask yourself is, "*Am I teaching out of theory, or am I experiencing the truth I am teaching?*" Learning begins with you as you apply the truth of the lesson to your life. Avoid at all cost the old adage, *Do as I say, not as I do.* First, you will look phony. Second, you will know nothing of what you are talking about. Third, you will not be sensitized to helping your students go through the learning process and the struggles of applying the truth to their lives. But if you have been trusting God to help you apply it to your life, you will be an expert at helping your learners.

PLANNING YOUR LESSON

The next important principle in good teaching is making sure you are prepared for your study time. Planning is the key.

1. The first step in planning is completing the study for that week yourself. That's right. Sit down and *work through the study.* Do so four or five days before your meeting. This gives you time to think about and apply the truth.
2. When you have completed the study, then begin your *lesson plan.* Your lesson plan involves these three elements.

a) Determine the *central truth* of the study. This is the main fact you want your students to learn from this lesson.
b) Establish your *goals*. Ask yourself the question, "By the end of this study, I want my students to be able to. . . ."
c) Determine the *needs of individual students*. If your group is small, list the specific truth you want each student to understand as a result of this study. If your group is larger, do this exercise for different students each week. You will find it to be very helpful in maintaining a person-centered perspective, rather than a perspective that is material-centered. It will help you to be very practical as you lead your students. It will give you specific needs to remember as you pray privately for your students.

3. The third element to your plan is developing your *teaching plan*. This is your plan of how you want to lead your students to an understanding and application of the facts being taught in the study.

   Break your teaching plan down into three segments:

   a) How will you *approach* the study? In other words, how will you get their attention and bring their minds to where their bodies are? How will you help them begin to focus on the central truth of the study?

      This is where short learning activities, three to six minutes, are well used. For a complete list of learning activities, purchase a copy of *Bible Learning Activities for Youth*, Gospel Light Publications, Ventura, CA 93006.

      Examples of learning activities include small buzz groups, a debate, skits, slide show, role playing, brainstorming, circle response, story writing, panel, songwriting, and many many others that are included in the book mentioned above. As you select learning activities, be sure they *relate directly to the central truth* of the study.

b) How will you help your students *understand the truth* of the study? This is the second element of your teaching plan. This is where you use *discussion and more learning activities* to help clarify the main points of the study. This is a time when students can also give feedback and ask questions. Here are some ideas that will help bring out and clarify the main points of the lesson. (It is best for each student to complete the lesson before he comes to the group.)
   - *Work through the content and questions* in the study and *discuss* the different responses of the students. These questions have been designed specifically to make the students think and help them express themselves. Allow for a good feedback time.
   - Use *learning activities* that help them discover the truth—help them begin to see how the facts of this study relate to their everyday lives. Some examples: buzz groups, role playing, etc.
   - A third way to discuss the topic of study is through a *question/answer (guided discussion) time.* As a teacher, you can guide the students through the session with skillful questioning. You will have to spend time preparing the questions you want to use. Structure your questions in a way that will make the students think and will create interaction—maybe even controversy. Do not use yes/no questions. Use progressive questions that build to the con-

clusion—the central truth. Include questions already used in the lesson.

c) *Application time*—the most critical element of your teaching plan. How will you guide them in making a personal application of the truth? This is where learning takes place.

In each study of the *So You* series, you will find a *Putting It All Together* section. This will help the students make decisions and apply the truth of the lesson. There are also questions within the study designed for personal examination and application. Know where these questions are located and use them as tools to help the students in their application.

In many cases, you will also want to be prepared with your own application ideas. Help the student answer the question, "*How will I use this truth in my life this week?*" Have them write out their application and, at times, have them verbalize the plans.

Here are some writing activities that often help students with their application. Have them complete these statements:

- "If I were to take this lesson seriously, I would have to. . . ."
- "I really need to ask God to make a few changes in my life, such as. . . ."
- "I am like (the Bible character in the study) in that I. . . ."

Provide 3 x 5 cards for the students to record their responses.

4. *Evaluation.* After you have completed your meeting with your students, take time to determine the effec-

tiveness of your time together. Take some personal time after the group meeting to make notes of what could have been done differently—how effective were the learning activities, what worked well, etc. Which students need to be drawn out at your next meeting? What are some special needs of the students? Pray specifically for your students and ask the Holy Spirit to help them understand and apply the material. Keep an evaluation notebook. Evaluate again a week later—this time observing any changes in the lives of the students. During their sharing time at the beginning of the next meeting, ask for responses to last week's study, and experiences they have had in applying that study to their lives.

5. *Personal relationships.* Meet personally with your students between study times. If you have a large group, meet with different students each week. You can meet them personally or in pairs. Again, this is a good time to ask questions, counsel, and get a pulse for where they are spiritually, as well as in other areas of their lives. Have a Coke together, witness together, attend a special event, etc. These times are perhaps the most beneficial times you will have in teaching and training young Christians. It will help you tailor-fit your teaching. Remember, the environment in which the Holy Spirit works must include your personal relationships with your students.

In conclusion, a *well-prepared teacher* is one who:

- Has been *preparing* for the study throughout the week and has not waited until the last minute to cram.
- Has determined the *central truth* and the goals of his study.

- Has thought through *a plan for helping his students understand* the truth of the lesson—learning activities, etc.
- Has thought through *a plan for helping his students apply* the truth of the study—application activities.
- *Evaluates* past sessions.
- Spends *personal time* with his students.
- *Prays* for his students.

SIX
A SAMPLE LESSON PLAN

Here is a sample lesson plan using the how to's we discussed in the previous chapter. This lesson plan is from chapter seven of *So You Want to Get into the Race:*

Meeting Date—October 21
Lesson 7—The Winning Quality

A. The *central truth* of this study is: Faith (putting our total trust in Christ and his Word) is the most important quality in a disciple's life. God builds our faith through our trials.
B. The *goal.* By the end of this meeting, my students should be able to:
   - List reasons why faith is the most important quality in a disciple's life.

- Understand how God produces faith in their lives.
- Have a positive attitude toward their trials.

C. *Individual needs* that can be met through this lesson. This week my special attention is on the needs of:

Ben—he tends to perform for God in a legalistic way. He needs to understand that his faith is what pleases God, not his works.

Michael and Joel—have been having some trials. This study will be a real help in giving them a perspective on their problems.

Cody—has been struggling with the idea of trusting God with his problems with Susan. This study will help him better understand the concept of faith.

Timothy—his father lost his job. This study will help Tim understand the gift of trials.

MY TEACHING PLAN

Materials and props I will need—blackboard and chalk.

A. *My Approach*—I will bring their attention to the study by:
- Brainstorming—write question on board, "The way to please God is by. . . ." Have each student give his answer. Do not evaluate the answers. The aim is quantity, not quality.
- Word association—ask them, "When you hear the word 'trust,' what comes to your mind?" Get verbal responses. Have everyone share. Take five minutes.

B. *Discovery and Discussion.* I will begin with buzz groups. Buzz groups—in groups of three discuss the question at top of page 67. Have them come to a unified decision and have group leaders share with entire group. Be sure to have them state why they came to their decision. Take ten minutes.

- Paraphrase of James 1:2-4 on page 70. Have several read their paraphrases. Have Tim read his to draw him out. As a group, have them discuss any particular trials they are experiencing right now. Ask them to describe what God has been teaching them through their trials. In what ways has it built their faith? Take ten to twelve minutes.

C. *Application Time.*
- Have each of them fill out the thought questions on pages 71-72. Discuss the questions on 72. Have each one give his answer to the last question, "The most significant thing I have learned in this study is. . . ." Take fifteen minutes.
- Pray for each other.
- Give assignment for this week.
- Don't forget—after the meeting, set up a Coke appointment with Cody for Wednesday afternoon. Invite Michael and Al to go to the game with you Monday night.

D. *Evaluation.*
Word association worked well.
Buzz groups took longer than I expected.
Discussion of trials went very well.
Michael and Joel got the picture.
Tim wants me to get together with his dad and share some of these truths with him personally.

SEVEN
PUTTING TOGETHER THE LOOSE PIECES

Here are several additional guidelines that you will find most helpful in leading your group or class.

- Ask that the students complete the studies before the group meeting. This will make the discussion and application time much more effective. It will also give you the freedom to use learning activities to help the students relate more personally to the facts of the study.
- However, ask the students not to complete the *Putting It All Together* section at the end of each study. This section is best used in your group meeting to help the students apply the lesson truth.
- Get excited when the students share ideas and give input. Be sure not to be critical of wrong answers. Correct gently.

- Always be sure to relate your learning activity to the lesson.
- If a particular chapter in a *So You* book covers more information than you feel your students should handle in one session, do not hesitate to break a chapter into two or more sessions. The bold-lettered subtitles throughout each chapter make good breaking points. Each subtitle begins a new thought.
- Ask each person in your group to buy a book. Not only do they need one, but it will make their commitment to the group more meaningful if it costs them something. The investment is minimal compared to what they are getting. If someone cannot afford a book, put together a fund through your church or organization that can help subsidize the cost.
- Always be very positive with your students. They want a leader who leads and who believes in them.

WHAT IF . . .

I know the thoughts that are troubling your mind. What if no one does the study? What if no one wants to talk about the study? Let's talk about some creative responses to this and some of the other "what if" problems.

- *What if several people forget their books?*

Have them share books. It is also good to have some extra books on hand.

- *What if they have not done their lessons?*

The type of lesson planning shown in this book allows you to teach the study even if some or all of the students do not complete their studies, but the effectiveness of your time together will be hindered. If this gets to be a problem, review with them the requirements for being part of the group which were outlined earlier in this book.

If they have not completed the lesson, have them do the lesson in pairs and then go directly to the *Putting It All Together* section. Or use your entire lesson plan the next week.

- *What if a number of people do not show up?*

Go ahead with your plans. If only one or two people are present, consider it a good time to personalize your relationship with them. If you cannot use your planned activities, be flexible. Lead a guided discussion. Above all, do not speak negatively of those who did not come.

- *What if people are late?*

Take a few moments to brief them, and have them join in.

- *What if they want to talk about something other than the lesson?*

Statements like, "I think we are off the subject. For the sake of time, why don't we get back on the subject?" will help you get back on track. If the subject they are talking about is important, and they all want to talk about it, make a note and cover that subject at a later time.

- *What if you do not get through your lesson plan?*

At your next meeting, review what you covered the week before, and complete the rest of the study. Or, if you see you are not going to have time to complete the study, go to your application time. If you continually have trouble completing your lesson in the time you have allotted, make adjustments in the amount of material you are trying to cover.

How to Use the So You Books

HOW TO USE SO YOU WANT SOLUTIONS

So You Want Solutions is written and designed for these specific audiences:

- *High school, junior high and college students. Small or large groups.*
- *Those who have recently received Christ.* This book helps the new Christian establish himself in the very basic truths of his Christian faith. It can be used in classes for young Christians, for individual follow-up, or for personal study.
- *Older Christians who have been involved in your ministry but need a better grounding in the basics of the Christian life.*
- *Individuals who have expressed an interest in the Christian life but have not yet made a decision to receive Christ.*

Chapters one and two are designed to communicate to those who have not received Christ, as well as to Christians. You can use chapters one and two to help introduce an individual to Christ and then use the remainder of the book for follow-up to help establish him in his faith. For Christians, chapters one and two help an individual confirm his decision for Christ and understand his decision more clearly.

FLOW OF THE BOOK

So You Want Solutions can actually be divided into two segments. Chapters one through five help a student better establish and understand his relationship with Christ. Chapters six through eleven help him grow in his relationship with Christ.

If you are working with one or more young Christians, and you feel they would more likely respond to a study group with a duration of five studies rather than eleven studies, here is a suggestion. Challenge them with the opportunity of meeting to discuss chapters one through five. When these chapters are completed, you can challenge them to a new commitment of six studies and go on to complete the book. Two shorter commitments are often better received by students who are new in the Body of Christ and are not yet accustomed to the consistent group-study idea. If a student should decide not to continue through the second six studies, he still will have the book for personal study. Obviously, this idea will not be necessary if you are using the book as part of your Sunday school curriculum, youth group studies, etc.

So You Want Solutions is a tool, and a good craftsman is creative in how he uses his tools.

SO YOU WANT SOLUTIONS—CHAPTER BY CHAPTER

This chapter-by-chapter overview is designed to help you as you put together your lesson plans. (See section entitled *How to Plan for Your Meeting.*)

For each chapter there are several suggestions that will help your students understand and apply the truth of the chapter. Select only those ideas that you feel apply best to your group, and please be creative in developing ideas of your own. This guide is designed only to stimulate your thought, not to give you a complete lesson plan. That is your job and it gives you an opportunity to personalize your teaching. Feel free to divide any of these chapters into two or more sessions if you see that it is necessary for adequately covering the material with your group. One idea is to discuss the content one week, and cover the application the next week. *Use the illustrations* in the chapters to emphasize a truth or for topics of discussion.

CHAPTER ONE—WHAT'S THE BUZZ ABOUT JESUS?
Central Truth. Jesus Christ is not only the greatest personality of history, he is also God.

Purposes. Someone has said, the heart cannot rejoice in what the head rejects. In other words, students do not get excited over something that they do not understand intellectually. They don't trust someone they don't know. In chapter one we help the student think through the most basic question of his Christian life: Who is Jesus Christ? This sets the foundation for his relationship with Christ, and it gives an apologetic for his faith.

Emphasis for Understanding.

- The first questions on page 10 are key for helping your students become personally involved in the central truth. It is the first step in helping them put "their fingerprints" on the study. Encourage personal opinions and discussion.
- In the sections *God Makes a Personal Appearance*

and *Did You Hear What He Said?* (pages 11 and 12), Scriptures are included that are key in understanding Christ's deity. Ask the students to select one of those passages and memorize it before your next meeting.

- Discuss the alternatives to Christ's identity given by C. S. Lewis on pages 12 and 13. Why couldn't Jesus have been a liar or a lunatic? Why is it reasonable to accept him as Lord? Ask for personal opinions.
- A key verse for discussion and memorization is John 20:31.

Activities for Application.

- What have students learned in this study that has strengthened their faith in Christ? Why has it strengthened their faith?
- What have they learned in this study that will help them communicate Christ to others? Have them verbalize their response.
- How will this study help students with other students on their campus, or with others at work?
- The poster activity on page 14 is designed to help the students recall the facts they learned about Christ, and relate them as they would communicate to their secular peers.
- Other activities you might use: Write a letter to a friend about the uniqueness of Jesus; interview a student who plays a part of a bystander from Jesus' time; have students write a TV news program reporting on Jesus Christ; have the students put together a graffiti poster illustrating everything they have learned from this study.

CHAPTER TWO—YOUR SOURCE OF SATISFACTION

Central Truth. Jesus Christ is the way to God and the source of true satisfaction.

Purposes. Many students know about Christ, but are unsure as to whether they really know him personally. This study helps Christians more firmly establish the fact that they have a personal relationship with Christ. For any non-Christians in your group, it simply and clearly explains how to receive Christ.

Don't assume anything with your students. You will be surprised at how many are unsure of their salvation and relationship with Christ. You will discover that there are some who have never received Christ. *This is a key to study.*

Emphasis for Understanding.

- Key question: top of page 16. This is their opportunity to put their fingerprints on the topic of study. Discuss their answers.
- Understanding sin is critical—see pages 17 and 18. Emphasize this section. Use a learning activity such as: Complete this statement, "Sin is. . . ." Play the devil's advocate—"sin is not a big issue." Let your students react or respond.
- Understanding what it means to receive Christ is the bottom line of this study. See pages 19 to 20. Have students discuss this section in buzz groups or in pairs.
- Key question: top of page 20. Have Christians share their personal testimonies. It's helpful for them to verbalize their relationship with Christ. Do not be hesitant to ask the students to verbalize this important issue. It is a great tool for spiritual growth.
- If there are non-Christians in your group, you could: (1) Have a silent moment for them to receive Christ, if that is their desire. Ask those who want to receive Christ to read the prayer (page 20) silently to God. Then after a few minutes, you can say a short prayer

of thanks. Explain that it is not the words of the prayer that are important but the attitude of their hearts. (2) You can later meet personally with those who you think may not be Christians and help them one on one.

Activities for Application.

- The *Putting It All Together* section is well designed to help the students apply the truth of this study. Don't be hesitant to ask students to verbalize their answers.
- Additional activity: Have students write a short personal testimony of why, when, and how they received Christ, and have it ready by the next meeting.

CHAPTER THREE—UNDERSTANDING YOUR NEW LIFE

Central Truth. Our faith in Christ is based on the promises (facts) of God's Word, Christ's continuous presence in our lives, and his gift of eternal life.

Purposes. Christians, new and old, need a clear understanding of who they really are because they have received Jesus Christ. Faith is grounded in these facts, and students who falter in their Christian walk usually do so because they do not have a clear understanding of the facts of their new identity. This study communicates these most basic facts.

Emphasis for Understanding.

- Here are the key truths emphasized in this chapter. Use learning activities to emphasize one or more of these truths.

1. Revelation 3:20 (top of page 22). The presence of Christ in your life.
2. 2 Corinthians 5:17 (page 22). Our new identity in Christ. Emphasize that we are no longer the old person we used to be, but that we are actually a new creation, and we will find our new meaning in life by building our relationship with Christ and learning to trust him with our needs.
3. Hebrews 13:5-8 (page 23). The promise of Christ's unconditional and continual presence in our lives.

- Our faith is based on fact, not on our feelings about the facts (pages 24 to 25). Emphasize this by having your students draw original illustrations or present a short skit to communicate this truth.
- A question for discussion groups, buzz groups, etc.—which of the truths from this study strengthens your faith the most? Why? Give all students a chance to respond verbally.

Activities for Application.

- The *Putting It All Together* section has two good application activities—a quick quiz and letter writing. Have students verbalize answers and read letters.
- To help students apply this truth, have them complete this statement, "If I were to take this study seriously, I would have to. . . ."

CHAPTER FOUR—
WHAT'S SO GOOD ABOUT GOOD FRIDAY?

Central Truth. Our forgiveness, our new life, and our acceptance from God would be impossible apart from Christ's death.

Purposes. It is difficult to appreciate Christ and our relationship with him unless we first understand our condition without him. This is often the problem in the Body of Christ—a deemphasis on sin and the condition of man apart from God.

This can be the source of many problems in a Christian's walk—disobedience, carnality, poor self-image, etc.

When we know what we have been saved from, and the price that has been paid, we get a lot more excited about the Savior. This study takes a simple but clear look at the significance of Christ's sacrifice and God's unconditional acceptance.

Emphasis for Understanding.

- The key Scripture at top of page 28 is Isaiah 59:2.
- Sin is *serious business* (pages 28 to 29). Suggested learning activities to emphasize this truth: Graffiti poster on how sin affects mankind, or how sin affects their campus; write a news story on a current event, and describe how man's sin contributes to the problem (see point three, page 28).
- Key question on page 31—have several students share their answers.
- Have students break up in two's and write a story similar to the example on pages 30 and 31—to communicate justice and forgiveness.
- God's acceptance (pages 32 to 33). Discuss reasons why we can know we are totally accepted by God. Discuss how this acceptance can make a difference in someone's self-image. Discuss significance of 2 Corinthians 5:21 and Colossians 1:22.

Activities for Application. In the *Putting It All Together* section, emphasize the application activity of sharing God's love with two people that day. Have students suggest ways they could share God's love.

- Have them finish this statement: "The truth in this study that has influenced me the most is. . ."
- Review the application project on page 26. This is an excellent place to have an introductory training session on how to share Christ with others.

CHAPTER FIVE—
YOU CAN'T KEEP A GOOD MAN DOWN

Central Truth. Christ's resurrection is a fact of history and this historical truth makes the Christian life a reality.

Purposes. Students need hooks upon which they can hang their faith—intellectual answers for those who question. In chapter one we covered a basic apologetic for understanding the Christian life—the uniqueness of Jesus. In this study we cover a second apologetic—*the evidences of the resurrection of Christ.* Remember the adage—*the heart cannot rejoice over what the head rejects.* The resurrection is another central truth for the Christian life, and in this study we discuss the evidence for this truth and its implications. You will find your students responding well to this study. Students are looking for intellectual support for their faith.

Emphasis for Understanding.

- The first question on page 36 gives special emphasis to 1 Corinthians 15:14-19. This lays the foundation for the importance of the resurrection. Use a learning activity here such as buzz groups, a panel, etc., to discuss this section.
- The learning activity at the top of page 39 (Complete the statement.) is key in helping you determine what the students can recall. Have them share their statements.

Activities for Application.

- The significance of the resurrection in our personal lives is the essential part of this study. To emphasize the information on pages 39 and 40, you will want to use another application activity. Suggestions: Complete this statement, "Christ's resurrection is important to me because. . . ."; or have them draw a picture to express what the resurrection means to them personally.
- Use the newspaper article activity on page 41 to help them think through the evidences and implications of the resurrection. If time does not allow, have them work on their articles during the week, and ask them to read their articles at your next meeting.

CHAPTER SIX—THE PERSON INSIDE

Central Truth. God lives in us in the person of his Holy Spirit, and we experience the Spirit's power as we learn to abide in Christ.

Purposes. Christianity, in the minds of many, is equated with a certain life style, tradition, and standard for living. Some of these are genuine results of the Christian life, but Christianity is much more unique than a particular life style. It is the actual indwelling of the person of Christ in the individual's life. Apart from this fact, the Christian life style would be an impossibility.

Young Christians, therefore, need to focus their attention, not so much on their behavior, but rather on the one who can change their behavior. This is the beginning of true Christian living—the true Christian walk. In this study we introduce the students to the biblical concept of the indwelling Spirit and the concept of dependence upon Christ and his Spirit (Romans 8:9). This sets the foundation for the next three studies.

Emphasis for Understanding.

- Have your students give illustrations explaining the Holy Spirit.
- Use the learning activity at the end of point four (page 45) to help the students recall the facts they discovered concerning the Holy Spirit. If they completed their paragraph before the meeting, give them a quick quiz.
- On pages 45 to 47, we use the familiar passage from John 15 to teach the biblical concept of abiding in Christ. Activities you could use to help the students personalize this truth are: graffiti posters; drawing a picture that depicts abiding in Christ; dividing them into pairs and having them think of illustrations of total trust (example—page 47) and share their illustrations with the group.
- The key to this study is helping the students learn what trust and faith really involve.

Activities for Application. Use the questions and activities on page 48 to help the students apply the truth being taught. When you meet personally with your students, ask them to share how they finished the statement, "If I were to take this study seriously, I would have to. . . ." Help them with suggestions for following through on their own commitment.

CHAPTER SEVEN—LIVING LIKE A WINNER

Central Truth. The Holy Spirit empowers us to live the Christian life. We are filled by the Spirit as the result of our faith. We demonstrate our faith by an act of our will.

Purposes. When it comes to teaching young Christians how to *walk with Christ,* there is no truth more important than the *ministry of the Holy Spirit.* The Holy Spirit makes the Christian walk possible. He empowers us to do God's will and leads us through our Christian adventure. The New Testament actually teaches that it is normal for a Christian to be filled with the Spirit. It is abnormal not to be filled with the Spirit.

In this study we want to communicate just what it means to be Spirit-filled, and we want to take a close look at some of the practical reasons why, at times, we do not experience the Spirit-filled life.

Emphasis for Understanding.

- Be creative in using learning activities. The ministry of the Holy Spirit is actually quite simple, but because it is based upon faith, and not works, it can be difficult to grasp at first.
- Understanding that the desires of our flesh are a problem, even though we are new creations in Christ, is critical to this study. Use a learning activity such as: Draw a picture that depicts or illustrates carnality or illustrates Galatians 5:17; have the students put together a skit or do role playing that would help the other students visualize the difference between the desires of our flesh and the fruit of the Spirit—pages 50 to 52.
- The question on page 52, "Which spiritual qualities are starting to develop in your life?" is the key to helping your students focus on the results of their walk with Christ. In other words, we should not desire the Spirit-filled life just to avoid carnality, but rather to experience the things that God has already planned for us—namely, his spiritual fruit.
- The four principles on pages 52 to 54 are the next important element in this study. This is not a formula, but rather the principles to follow as we

pursue our Spirit-filled life. These principles do not involve works for which you will receive some kind of spiritual credit, but they are attitudes and actions that involve an act of our will. We must be willing to confess, etc. Use a learning activity to help the students recall these four principles. Suggestions: Quick quiz; graffiti posters; matching Scriptures to principles.

- Be sure to emphasize the difference between our faith and our feelings on page 55. Have students draw their own illustration that would communicate this difference.

Activities for Application

- Have each of them personally think through and answer the three questions in the *Putting It All Together* section. At times it is good to have the students individually and privately list areas of their lives where they have been disobedient to God. Before God, they can then confess these areas of sin and claim God's forgiveness according to 1 John 1:9. Have them write 1 John 1:9 across their list, and then destroy the paper.
- In the next chapter the students will again review the main truths of this lesson.

CHAPTER EIGHT—WALKING IN THE SPIRIT

Central Truth. In the same way that we trust the Holy Spirit to fill us (by our faith), we can go on trusting him for power to live our Christian lives day by day and moment by moment.

Purposes. The practical test of the ministry of the Holy Spirit in a Christian's life is learning to trust the Spirit's leadership. The real test comes when things are especially difficult.

If students are going to understand this great truth, we must be practical, we must be living it ourselves, and we must not be critical of our students' failures. The young always crawl before they walk, and they always walk before they run.

Emphasis for Understanding.

- Review the questions under *Walking a New Route* (page 58). This will stimulate good discussion and review the central truths of the last study.
- The key to understanding the Spirit-filled life is made clear for us in Galatians 5:16 (see pages 59 to 60). Many of us want to first "clean up our act" before we think we can be filled with God's Spirit. If you think about that, it's a bit foolish. If we could clean up our act, we wouldn't need the Spirit. Rather, as we humble ourselves before God, confess our sin, and claim the Spirit's power, we will then have the Spirit's resources to live a fruitful life and not carry out the desires of the flesh. Ask the students to give their answers and reasoning to the questions on the top of page 60. Good for buzz group discussion.
- In the section entitled *Let's Be Realistic,* ask your students to share similar experiences. This helps them identify with the problems.
- Good discussion questions for the entire group or for buzz groups are brought out on page 62. Why is it wrong for a Christian to sit around and feel guilty when he sins? Why does guilt alienate us from God? Have them share an experience of how guilt has alienated them from another person who actually loved them.

Activities for Application.

- The letter writing activity on page 63 is designed to help the students express what they have learned. Have several read their letters aloud.

CHAPTER NINE—GETTING INTO THE WORD

Central Truth. God's Word is our main source of spiritual food. It builds our faith and equips us for his service. God asks us not only to feed on his Word, but more important, to obey it.

Purposes. The purpose of this study is to help motivate young Christians to personally read, study, and apply the Word. In Colossians 3:16 Paul tells us, "Let the word of Christ dwell in you richly (NIV)." In Hebrews 4:12, we read, "The Word of God is living and active. Sharper than any double-edged sword, it penetrates even to dividing soul and spirit . . . it judges the thoughts and attitudes of the heart (NIV)." Apart from a steady diet of the Word of God, spiritual growth in the lives of our students is an impossibility.

Emphasis for Understanding.

- Do a *rebus* of 2 Timothy 3:16. Have each student substitute a word or a symbol for every word they can in 2 Timothy 3:16.
- Stimulation question for discussion or buzz groups: How has the Word helped you in your Christian growth (page 66)? Have them give examples.
- To help students personalize the truth on pages 68 and 69, ask them to do the exercise on the bottom of page 69. Ask them to list two specific things that God has recently shown them in his Word, and how they have attempted to apply those truths in their lives. Have them do this on paper or verbally in groups.

Activities for Application.

- Select a passage from the Word, such as John 15:1-8, or Colossians 3:12-17, and have them do a Bible study using the guidelines on page 70 and the notebook layout on page 71. This will help them get acquainted with this study method.

- Have them share the things they discovered in their Bible study, either as a group or in smaller buzz groups.
- When you meet personally with your students, discuss what they are learning in their Bible study times. Help them find regular time to get into the Word and start a Bible study notebook.

CHAPTER TEN—COMMUNICATING WITH GOD

Central Truth. Prayer is the great privilege we have to express ourselves to a listening God. Prayer builds our intimate relationship with our Lord.

Purposes. In our last study we discussed God's primary method of communicating with his children—by his Word. In this study, we are going to discuss the method by which we communicate with God—prayer.

Prayer is looked at by many as a very difficult discipline, almost work. It's no wonder so few people pray. In this study we want to communicate the positive privilege as well as the positive results of prayer.

Emphasis for Understanding.

- You could begin your session by asking each student to verbalize one need they would want God to meet. Then compare these needs to the Scripture under *Does Prayer Really Make a Difference?* Have the students give you the promises of these Scriptures, and list them on the board.
- To help them recall the principles under *How Does God Want Us to Pray?*, use a learning activity. Suggestions: A skit or role play dramatizing a father and his son or daughter. The child wants to ask the parent

for something but must follow the principles. A second suggestion would be a quick quiz on the three principles.

- Emphasize and discuss the role of faith (believing God) in our prayer life. Lack of faith is usually the biggest reason we do not pray (page 75).
- Emphasize the question on the bottom of page 76. Have the students discuss examples of waiting for an answer to prayer, and how waiting has helped them grow spiritually. Be creative with this point. One of the biggest reasons Christians fail to pray is that they do not understand unanswered prayer.
- Help them plan a time for prayer—usually the same time they study the Word. However, many find it good to spend time in prayer in the morning and in the Word in the evening, or vice versa.

Activities for Application.

- In addition to the *Putting It All Together* section, encourage each of the students to start a prayer notebook or diary listing their prayer requests and God's answers.
- Have them complete this statement, "The most significant truth I have learned in this study is. . . ." Or have them complete this statement, "The best way that I can apply this study to my life is by. . . ."

CHAPTER ELEVEN—THE IMPORTANCE OF OTHERS

Central Truth. Our relationships with others, both Christians and non-Christians, are essential to our spiritual growth. Christ has given us the privilege of sharing his love with others.

Purposes. Bible study and prayer are essential to growth. These are the "feeding" elements of spiritual development, so to speak. Now we have come to two more essentials—nonnegotiables. First, our active involvement in the Body of Christ. Second, our involvement in a ministry to others. Both are absolutely essential if we are to grow spiritually.

Again, we want to provide a positive picture of what it means to be active in the Body of Christ. And, of course, we want to provide a very positive picture of personal evangelism.

Emphasis for Understanding.

- Under *God's Family Plan* (page 80), you could use a learning activity to discuss how the Body of Christ meets the spiritual needs of individuals. Suggestions: Panel, skits, etc.
- In buzz groups or with a panel, discuss how we can be more involved in the ministry of our local church. Perhaps you could have your pastor come to your group and discuss the opportunities in your local body.
- Under *Those Who Have Not Received Christ,* have several students who were led to Christ one-on-one share their experiences. This would have a great effect on the other students, and will motivate them to share their faith.
- Use a learning activity to help them recall the four principles for sharing their faith (pages 81 to 85). Suggestions: Quick quiz, graffiti poster.

Activities for Application.

- Have students complete a list of names on the bottom of page 84.
- When you come to the question, "How will you share your faith?" have the students role play. One will share Christ, and one will be the listener—the

non-Christian. Have your other students respond to the role play and ask for suggestions for improving communications in their evangelism.

- Discuss the different ways or methods by which your students could share their faith with others.
- Offer a training seminar on how to share one's faith. This is a good opportunity to teach your students how to use evangelistic tools such as *Steps to Peace With God* (Billy Graham Association, Minneapolis, MN 55440), *Four Steps Up* (Open Door Press, Box 13619, St. Louis, Missouri) or *The Four Spiritual Laws* (Campus Crusade for Christ, San Bernardino, California 92414).

YOUR GROWTH INVENTORY

You may want to spend an entire session reviewing the students' answers and responses to this inventory, or you may want to meet with them one on one, and go over it together.

Purposes.

1. Students like to express themselves. This is their opportunity.
2. This is also your opportunity to evaluate their growth and get a good look at what's happening in their lives. It is a very healthy and productive activity. You can use group discussion, buzz groups, etc.
3. This inventory also gives you help in determining what is best for their future spiritual development.

At the completion of this inventory challenge each student to a new involvement with you and a new series of studies. *So You Want to Get into the Race* and *So You Want to Set the Pace* are books available in this series.

TWO
HOW TO USE
SO YOU WANT TO GET INTO THE RACE

So You Want to Get into the Race is written and designed for these specific audiences:

- High school students, college students, and young adults. It is very effective with a wide range of ages. It can be used with large groups, small discipleship groups, or for personal study.
- Students whom you want to begin to disciple personally.
- Christians who have had some teaching in Christian basics and have a hunger to learn more and continue to grow in their spiritual lives. This book is very helpful to those who are sensitive in their walk with Christ and who want to be liberated from the problems of legalism and performance for God.

PURPOSE OF THE BOOK

So You Want to get into the Race takes a practical look at spiritual growth and the steps of discipleship. Although this book deals with several of the same subjects as *So You Want Solutions,* it takes the student deeper into these subjects and requires more application.

If you like to challenge students and make them think, this book is for your ministry. If you are young as a ministry leader, and just learning to challenge students, this book will be of great value to you also. In fact, it will challenge your students for you.

Challenging and encouraging make up the backbone of Christian ministry. Jesus challenged individuals with spiritual truth, and encouraged them with his love. When we ask students to be honest with God, and with themselves, we are providing the environment they need for their spiritual growth. When we love them, we are helping them to blossom.

FLOW OF THE BOOK

The first two chapters of *So You Want to Get into the Race* establish basic premises for the studies—*who is a disciple,* and *what does the Lord ask of him?* From there we take an exciting journey through the most profound truths of the Christian disciple's life—his *position* with Christ, his *identity* in Christ, his *power* in Christ, and his *purpose* in Christ. We have taken great care in presenting these truths in a practical, down-to-earth manner. The purpose of these studies is to help students *experience* these biblical truths, not just intellectualize them.

The remainder of the book, chapters seven through nine, then brings the students to a very practical look at their own problems and trials as a disciple, and the influences upon their mind in a messed-up world. The book ends with an emphasis on the personal study of God's Word and a challenge to reevaluate priorities.

So You Want to Get into the Race is a tool, and the good craftsman is creative in how he uses his tools.

SO YOU WANT TO GET INTO THE RACE—
CHAPTER BY CHAPTER

This chapter-by-chapter overview is designed to help you as you construct your lesson plans (see chapter five).

For each chapter there are several suggestions that will help your students understand and apply the truth of the chapter. Select only those ideas that will apply best to your group, and please be creative in developing ideas of your own. This guide is designed only to stimulate your thought, not give a complete lesson plan. That is your job and it gives you an opportunity to personalize your own teaching. Take adequate time to study each chapter on your own.

Feel free to divide any of these chapters into sections if you see that it is necessary in order to adequately cover the material with your group. One idea is to discuss the content of the study one week, and cover the application the next week. *Use the illustrations* in the chapters to emphasize truth and for topics of discussion.

Encourage your students to work through the Scripture passages for personal study at the end of each chapter. These are designed for mid-week study between your group meetings. When you meet with them personally, discuss what they are learning in their personal study of the Word.

The *Putting Together Your Priorities* section at the end of the book is a project that can be used at any time in the progression of your group. It is a tool for helping young disciples evaluate their priorities and organize their time.

CHAPTER ONE—RELIGION OR RELATIONSHIP
Central Truth. Discipleship in its most basic form, is developing a personal relationship with Jesus Christ.

Purposes. There is no question that Christians have varied opinions about discipleship. Some describe disciples exclusively as those who are mature Christians. That's a nice idea except for one problem—determining the point at which an individual actually moves from just being a Christian to actually becoming a disciple. The Scriptures do not make this clear. However, what the Scriptures do make clear is the distinct event in each of our lives that gives us the assurance that we are children of God. Jesus said, "Anyone who believes . . ." becomes part of God's family (John 3:16).

This, according to the Scriptures, is the beginning point in any disciple's life. He has made a commitment to begin to trust Christ. Now he must involve himself in discipleship.

The emphasis of this chapter is that all Christians must look at themselves as basically being Christ's disciples. This is not an option. What is an option is a response to who we really are.

Are we willing to involve ourselves in discipleship—the growing process of a disciple? This is what Jesus has asked of us, and this is what he expects. But first, let's make sure we are Christians; then we can begin the discipleship journey.

In addition to defining a disciple, this chapter will also be helpful to those individuals in your group who may not have the personal assurance that they have received Christ. Spend special time with these individuals and help them think through their personal relationship with Christ. There may be some people in your group who have not received Christ.

Emphasis for Understanding.

- Question for arousing discussion—top of page 10. When you allow people to share their opinions, it always gets them involved in the study. They will stick with you to compare their opinions to the facts.
- You could also approach your session with a word association game: "When I say the word 'disciple,' what comes to your mind?" Allow all to respond and give an opinion.
- You could use a learning activity to describe and compare the different characters identified in the Scriptures on pages 10 and 11. Suggestions: Spontaneous role play—have students act out the way they think a certain character in these Scriptures would have presented himself if asked if he/she were a disciple of Jesus. Discuss how we sometimes present ourselves. What effect does our behavior have on determining who we really are? If we know who we really are, should that affect our behavior?
- Questions on page 12 can be used three ways:
  1. To help clarify students' definition of a Christian.
  2. To help students think through their personal experience of receiving Christ.
  3. To help you to determine who in your group is unsure of his relationship with Christ.
- Be sure to meet personally with any individuals who may have questions about their salvation.
- Use a learning activity to emphasize the definition of discipleship on page 14. A suggestion would be a quick quiz, having them write the definition down from memory. Make sure your disciples understand and memorize this definition.

Activities for Application.

- The relationship inventory on pages 15 through 16 is designed to help your students personally think through the condition and growth of their relationship with Jesus Christ. Have them go through it and discuss their responses. This tool is also designed for one-on-one interaction with your disciples.

CHAPTER TWO—WINNING ATTITUDES

Central Truth. Right attitudes are the basic requirement that Christ asks of every disciple. To grow as a disciple, three attitudes are essential—*availability, teachability, faithfulness.*

Purposes. The purpose of this study, and the next three, is to help students begin discipleship on the right foot. In the first chapter, we discussed who we are by God's love and grace. (He has given us the privilege to be his disciples.) Now we are going to discuss our response to his love. What does he want us to do? Where do we begin? How can we demonstrate our response to him? The answer—it begins with *right attitudes.*

Emphasis for Understanding.

- The question on the bottom of page 17 is designed to help the students get involved in the study—bring their minds together with their bodies.
- This study has commitment (application) activities at the end of each discussion of the three winning attitudes (pages 20, 22, and 24). Use these as group discussion questions, buzz group questions, etc. Or the students could pair off to interview each other and discover their thoughts and commitments concerning the questions.

- Use a learning activity or sharing time to discuss different hindrances Christians have in making themselves available to Christ. See the illustration on page 19.
- Have students role play or act out their concept of a teachable person and a nonteachable person. Discuss examples of Christians being unteachable in relation to the Word of God. How can we demonstrate teachability?
- Have students discuss the truth they have learned and how they could be faithful in applying that truth. This could be done in large or small discussion groups.

Activities for Application.

- Have each student evaluate himself—page 24 and top of page 25.
- The questions on page 25 and the creative *contract* on page 26 are designed to help the students make clear commitments to the Lord and the group and to express their availability to you as their leader. Be sure to have them complete the contract.
- Have the students review and discuss the commitments they made in regard to the three winning attitudes (pages 20, 22, and 24).

CHAPTER THREE—MAN, HAVE I BLOWN IT!

Central Truth. When a Christian sins, the security of his relationship with God never changes, but the vitality and intimacy of that relationship is hindered. Confession is God's plan for restoring that vitality.

Purposes. Guilt is, without question, one of the biggest neutralizers of committed Christians. It's perhaps Satan's primary weapon against God's kids. Therefore, if we want our students to grow, we have to help them deal with sin and guilt. It's a nonnegotiable.

In this study we approach the problem from a very practical position—the position of who we really are in Jesus Christ. To some it may seem that teaching these truths is taking an unnecessary risk. We may fear that we are communicating a license to sin. For some who are less committed to Christ and understand less of his love, this could be true. With these people we must be firm on obedience, but at the same time help them clearly understand the unconditional love of God. For God's love and acceptance always produce a desire to obey.

However, students who have a desire to grow spiritually need this breath of fresh, liberating air. It could very well change some lives. This is one of the most significant teachings of the entire Bible.

Emphasis for Understanding.

- The question at the bottom of page 27 is designed to help the students bring their minds together with their bodies. Emphasize it.
- Emphasize the seriousness of sin in God's sight (*God Paid a Big Price*—page 28). This is key in understanding the rest of this chapter. At the beginning of your study (your approach) you could have each student give an example of how sin affects a Christian's life, his power, his joy, etc.
- The important fact to emphasize on pages 28 and 29 is that sin does not sever our relationship with God. Use a learning activity such as: A skit or role play of father and son. Son is disobedient to father. Does that mean that the son is not any longer related to the father? Have students discuss and relate it to their

relationship with their heavenly Father. What is different and what is similar about God's attitude towards disobedient children as compared to the attitude of a human parent?

- Discuss the illustration on the bottom of page 30. How does the way we see ourselves differ from the way God sees us? How should we see ourselves? Why? What does this do for our self-image? Why?
- Have students act out a court scene similar to the one on page 31.
- Make it clear that confession is not doing something for God, but accepting something that is already ours. See pages 32 to 34.
- Have them memorize the definition of confession. Give them a quick quiz to recall the definition.

Activities for Application.

- In buzz groups, or in pairs, have them work through their suggestions for counseling the boy with the problem on pages 34 and 35.
- Have the students privately go through the special project on page 36. Allow ten to fifteen minutes for this project.

CHAPTER FOUR—BUT I CAN'T LIVE THE LIFE

Central Truth. Trying to live the Christian life by the ability of our flesh (our natural abilities) is a losing cause—an impossibility. Rather, the Christian life is lived as we discover what it means to have been crucified with Christ and to live by faith in the Son of God.

Purposes. This is perhaps the most important chapter in this entire book. The cornerstone of Christian living is

Galatians 2:20. Christians, young and old, need to take this verse by the horns, wrestle with it, and begin to integrate it into their daily lives. It is a nonnegotiable if we want to equip our disciples for supernatural living.

Most of us are tired of struggling in our Christian lives . . . running in our own steam. *We need relief.* The uniqueness of this study is simply this: Instead of pointing us to one more thing we should *do* to be committed to Christ, it directs us back to the basics of who we are (our identity). It helps clarify, in a practical context, the fact of our death and resurrection with Christ. It focuses attention on the right things in the Christian life, not on those works that only stimulate the flesh.

It is important to understand that the truth of this lesson will later be balanced out with things we are to *do* in the Christian life—in chapters six, eight, and nine. In this chapter we first want to establish the truth of true spirituality. Once we are walking by faith, we can then add works that demonstrate our faith.

Emphasis for Understanding.

- I recommend that you read Romans 1—8, and the book of Galatians, before you teach this study. Give yourself time to think through these exciting Scriptures.
- Be creative in your approach. Help your students clearly see their need for this study. Suggestions: Ask for responses to the illustration on page 37. Why is the fellow tired out? What title or caption would you give the picture? Do you relate to him? How? Why?
- Our flesh is often aroused because of laws and rules (top of page 39). The flesh is a natural rebel. Under the section entitled *Why You Can't Live the Life,* discuss the story of the broken window. In buzz

groups have them come up with similar experiences from their own lives.

- Please take note of the last paragraph in this same section (page 40). Use a learning activity to discuss why we fail to do the good things we often attempt in our Christian lives. How does this work out in a real-life situation? Suggestions: Role play; interview; pair up students and have them write a short story or a parable that teaches this truth.
- A key to this entire study is in the section entitled *Your Identification, Please!* Suggested learning activities: Question on top of page 42—discuss it as a group or in buzz groups; play the devil's advocate and attack student's identity in Christ. Make them defend who they are; have them interview each other —one as the interviewer or reporter asking the other to identify himself and explain who he is in Christ.
- Suggested learning activities for the section entitled *Consider Yourself . . .* (pages 42 to 43): Have them draw a sketch or picture, design an advertisement brochure, or write a song that communicates this truth.

Activities for Application.

- In pairs or on their own, have students paraphrase Romans 8:3, 4 (page 43). Have different ones share their paraphrases. Use this to draw out less involved students.
- Discuss the remaining questions on pages 43 to 44. Have everyone give their response to the last statement. Do this as an entire group or, if your group is too large, have them do it in buzz groups of four or so.
- Be sure to emphasize the personal study Scriptures on page 44. This will help clarify the truth of the lesson.

CHAPTER FIVE—DOING WHAT COMES SUPERNATURALLY

Central Truth. As new creations in Christ, with a new identity, we now can live the powerful Christian life by being filled and led by the Holy Spirit.

Purposes. Many Christians lead mild to desperately boring lives. Many are defeated—no power. If you think about it, something isn't quite right. Jesus said, "My purpose is to give life in all its fullness" (John 10:10). Paul tells us, "I have strength for all things in Christ who empowers me" (Philippians 4:13, AMP). These Scriptures paint a picture that is often significantly different from what we experience.

This study is dedicated to those who are tired of mediocrity—vanilla Christian lives. We want to help our learners grasp a deeper understanding and personal application of the Spirit-filled life . . . the kind of life style that God intended for us to live.

This study builds on chapter four. We have established our identity in Christ. Now we are going to discuss the source of our spiritual power.

Emphasis for Understanding.

- Use the last question on page 46 for buzz groups. The Spirit-filled life and confession go hand in hand. Discuss the negative results if we choose not to confess.
- *Claim what is yours*—pages 47 to 48. The key here is accepting something that is already ours . . . a most critical truth of this study. Suggestions for learning: Have the students produce a skit or short drama that illustrates someone who has received a rich inheritance, but does not claim it. Others try to convince him, but he keeps giving excuses as to why he does

not want to accept it. Have students discuss how this attitude relates to our Christian lives.

- Learning to walk in the Spirit is the theme of this study
  (beginning with *Consider Yourself Dead*—page 48). Walking in the Spirit involves these two central principles:
  1. Reckoning yourself dead.
  2. Making choices which allow the Spirit to lead us.
- Suggested learning activities for the section entitled *Consider Yourself Dead:* To recall the truth in chapter four, have your students complete this statement, "To be crucified with Christ means. . . ." Or, have them continue the earlier inheritance drama. It should help them understand that once we know who we are, new creatures in Christ, it is natural for us to then allow the Holy Spirit to fill and lead us.
- Work through the section entitled *Making Choices* as a total group or as buzz groups. Emphasize the pie project on page 51.

Activities for Application.

- Have a time of silence for approximately ten minutes, and ask your students to work through the *Putting It All Together* Section on pages 53 and 54.
- The key application questions are on page 54. Have different students give their responses to the last two questions.

CHAPTER SIX—SUPERNATURAL RELATIONSHIPS

Central Truth. The fruit of the Spirit-filled life will not be experienced in a vacuum. Spiritual fruit and power become a reality when we involve ourselves in the lives of others.

Purposes. Have you ever asked yourself the question, "If I am Spirit-filled, why isn't there more evidence?" In this study we seek to be practical concerning this whole area of results in the Spirit-filled life. Why can't we just "lie back" and expect to see the Spirit produce fruit in our lives? What are some practical things we must do if we are going to put ourselves in a position where spiritual fruit will become a reality? The answers to these questions nearly always take us into relationships. This is the action of the disciple's life.

Emphasis for Understanding.

- To bring home the fact of the changed lives of Peter and John (pages 56 to 58), have the students: 1) Act out the ways they think these disciples would have acted in difficult or stressful situations; 2) complete this statement, "I am like (Peter or John) in that I. . . ."
- As a group or in buzz groups, discuss why relationships with non-Christians put us in a position where the fruit of the Spirit is absolutely essential.
- Compare the Peter and John of old (page 56) to the Peter and John of Acts 4. Suggestions: For each problem found in the Scriptures on page 56, find the change in that area of their lives as recorded in Acts 4; have the students share a specific area in their own lives where God has changed them; have the students draw contrasting sketches or pictures that illustrate the changes in the disciples' lives, and then their own lives.

Activities for Application.

- Discuss in groups how your local body of believers (your church) compares to the first church in the Book of Acts (see pages 61 to 63). Discuss positive action each person could take to make your body of believers more like those in Acts.
- Work through the *Putting It All Together* section as buzz groups or in pairs. Come back together, and

share the wealth of your ideas and the decisions for action.

CHAPTER SEVEN—THE WINNING QUALITY
For insights for this study, see the *sample lesson plan* (page 45) in the first portion of this book.

Purposes. Faith is the capstone as well as the foundation of a disciple's walk. In this study we bring the finishing touches to the last three chapters. This is a very practical look at faith and how God produces faith in our lives. You'll find this study especially helpful to those who are going through trials and difficulties.

CHAPTER EIGHT—A CHRISTIAN'S
MIND IN A MESSED-UP WORLD
Central Truth. As Christians there is an intense battle raging for control of our minds. The enemy is determined to neutralize our faith in Christ. The first step in winning the battle is to identify the enemy's strategy.

Purposes. In the previous chapters, our discussions of a disciple's life style culminated with the subject of our faith—the bottom line of Christian living. Now in chapters eight and nine, we are discussing the reality of keeping our faith vital and dynamic. This chapter brings a disciple's life style down to raw reality.

For more insight on this subject, read: *The Magic Bubble* by Pat Hurley (Wheaton, Illinois: Victor Books, 1978).

Emphasis for Understanding.
- For your approach ask the students, "What is one thing you have seen or heard on the radio or television in the last twenty-four hours that could hinder

your faith in Christ? Why?" If your group is small enough, have each student share his response. If it is a larger group, break up into pairs for two minutes.

- Have the students match the cartoons on pages 76 and 77 to the philosophies they illustrate.
- Give a quick quiz asking the students to list and explain the four philosophies that this study talks about.
- As a large group or in buzz groups, thoroughly discuss the questions under *Don't Be Taken Captive* and *Getting Personal* on pages 76 to 78.
- In pairs or buzz groups have the students discuss the Scriptures on page 79, then decide which philosophy the Scripture relates to and how it helps them deal with that philosophy.
- Ask each student to select one Scripture from page 79, and memorize that Scripture during the coming week. Ask them to share why they selected that particular Scripture.

Activities for Application.

- Discuss thoroughly the questions on page 80.
- Have students make plans for communicating Christ on their campuses or at their jobs. Help them think through simple but faith-stretching things they can do.
- In small groups have the students design a brochure, poster, or cartoon strip that would describe the world's philosophies and what a Christian should beware of.

CHAPTER NINE—USING THE SWORD OF THE SPIRIT

Central Truth. There are so many influences in the world seeking to mold us that it is essential that we hedge ourselves with the Word of God.

Purposes. This chapter is a natural sequence to chapter eight. We have identified the enemy's strategy. Now we bring out our heavy artillery—God's powerful Word.

This is an important study for two reasons. First, it points our students toward *the solution* in the battle for their minds. Second, it gives them practical *motivation* and "how to's" for continuing their intake of God's Word.

Emphasis for Understanding.

- Give a quick quiz asking your students to list the four philosophies talked about in chapter eight. This will bring their minds back to the subject and give motivation for this study.
- Have students draw their own sketch or picture to illustrate the importance of God's Word. Or, in pairs, have them list all the benefits of the Word and make an advertisement brochure or a book cover illustrating these benefits.
- Brainstorm—ask the students to list things that keep Christians from studying the Word. For each problem that keeps us from the Word, have them discuss a solution.
- Go over *A Simple Plan for Getting into the Word* (pages 84 to 86), and then give a quick quiz to help them recall the seven steps in this plan.

Activity for Application.

- Have each student go through the *Putting It All Together* section. This will help them experience the use of the study plan.
- Have them complete this statement, "The most significant truth I have learned in this study is. . . ."
- Have them complete this statement, "The way I intend to apply this study to my life is by. . . ."

PUTTING TOGETHER YOUR PRIORITIES

Purposes. Wrong priorities and wasted time are two reasons young disciples struggle in their walk with Christ. The Scriptures instruct us repeatedly to be wise in setting our priorities (Luke 9:23-25) and to use our time wisely (John 9:4).

This tool is designed to help your students think through their priorities as disciples and their time commitments. You can take an extra study session for this project, or have each student work through the project and then meet with him personally to go over his results and decisions. You can use this project at the completion of the book, or interject it at any point while going through the book.

As you continue to meet personally with your disciples, encourage them to stick with their priorities and schedules. There will be a rich return in their lives.

When you have completed this book, move on to the next book in the series, *So You Want to Set the Pace.* This tool is designed to help your students sharpen their involvement in the lives of others.

THREE
HOW TO USE
SO YOU WANT TO SET THE PACE

So You Want to Set the Pace is designed for these specific audiences:

- High school students, college students, young adults. It is effective with a broad range of ages, and it can be used in large groups, small discipleship groups, or for personal study.
- It is written for Christians who have a desire to learn the basics of ministering to others, i.e., leading others to Christ and helping them in their spiritual growth and development.
- A prerequisite for any individual using this book is an understanding of the basics in his Christian walk. He or she should have completed either *So You Want Solutions,* or *So You Want to Get into the Race,* or both.

PURPOSE OF THE BOOK

A friend once said to me, "Chuck, it's impossible to grow spiritually if you are not having a ministry in the lives of others." I didn't know how biblical his bold statement was, so I decided to dig in and take a look for myself. What did the Scriptures have to say?

I came across John 4. Jesus had just finished sharing with the Samaritan woman when his disciples returned with some food for their lunch. Instead of eating the food, Jesus made this interesting statement: "I have food to eat you know nothing about. . . . My food . . . is to do the will of him who sent me and to finish his work" (John 4:32, 34, NIV). What had Jesus done? Essentially he had been witnessing. And this step of obedience was his source of spiritual nourishment! *Getting involved in the lives of others really does cause spiritual growth.*

In my own life and in the lives of many I have had the privilege of working with, a personal ministry has been the turning point from spiritual mediocrity to a vital walk with the Lord. When you are giving out to others, the Lord just seems to provide for you. The spiritual growth of you and your students is one reason this book has been made available.

A second reason for this book, and even more important than the first, is the fact that God has commanded us to be laborers in his harvest. In Matthew 28:19 and Mark 16:15 Jesus made it very clear that we are to communicate the good news to everyone and to make disciples. In 2 Corinthians 5:10 Paul calls himself an ambassador for Christ, and this truth applies to our lives also. Being Christ's ambassador is not an option, it's a command, and *So You Want to Set the Pace* will help your students get their start in being faithful to our Lord's command.

FLOW OF THE BOOK

In the first two chapters we deal with the biblical basis for investing our lives in others. Who are we? We are new creations in Jesus Christ, created to do good works. Can we do these good works? Yes, we can, if we focus on our relationship with Christ and abide in him. That's the source of our spiritual fruit.

In chapter three we establish the first priority for our personal ministry—our homes. In chapters four through seven we then center on our ministry to nonbelievers—our witness and evangelism. In chapters eight and nine we discuss follow-up and helping young Christians grow. Chapter ten is a final challenge to a lifetime of ministry and a commitment to spiritual multiplication.

SO YOU WANT TO SET THE PACE—
CHAPTER BY CHAPTER

This chapter-by-chapter overview is designed to help you as you prepare your lesson plans. (See chapter five.) For each chapter I have listed several suggestions that will help your students understand and apply the truth of the chapter. Select only those ideas that you feel apply best to your group, and please be creative in developing ideas of your own. This guide is only designed to stimulate your thought, not to give a complete lesson plan. That is your job and it provides you with an opportunity to personalize your teaching.

Feel free to divide any of these chapters into two or more sessions if you see that it is necessary for adequately covering the material with your group. One idea is to discuss the content of the chapter one week, and go over the application at your next meeting. Use the illustrations in the chapters to emphasize truth and for topics of discussion. Encourage your students to work through the assigned Scriptures for personal study each week. This will help them understand more clearly the truth being taught.

At the end of each chapter there is a section entitled *My Action This Week.* These are assignments designed to help your students apply the principles taught in the lesson. Take time at each meeting to discuss these activities, and give clear directions for helping your students carry out the activities. The success of this book in the lives of your students is greatly dependent on these activities.

CHAPTER ONE—WHO ARE YOU?
Central Truth. As new creations in Jesus Christ, we will find meaning and satisfaction in walking with Christ and investing our lives in others.

Purposes. In this first chapter we establish a very basic fact of Christianity that I think is often underemphasized in Christian teaching. It is found in 2 Corinthians 5:17. If we have trusted our lives to Jesus Christ, we are *new creations in him.* This means that we have a new set of values and a new source of satisfaction. It also means that we have a new life style. There are new priorities to follow and new activities in which to be involved.

A big part of this new life style is ministering to others, meeting others' spiritual needs. For the Christian, doing anything else is just abnormal. In a very refreshing way we have moved personal ministry out of the realm of "extracurricular Christian activities" and moved it into the natural day-in and day-out experience. This, I am convinced, is the cornerstone of a proper and biblical motivation for ministry.

Emphasis for Understanding.
- Suggested learning activity to illustrate story about the basketball player (pages 9 and 10): Ask students

to share a personal experience of lacking confidence in doing something that eventually they found they could do very well. Why did they lack confidence? How did they discover they were capable of doing this particular thing? How did their self-concept change as a result? Have them do a self-evaluation. Give out 3 x 5 cards, and have them complete this statement, "When it comes to living the Christian life, I am like the basketball player in that I, too, ..."

- Discuss the last paragraph in the section *The Truth about You* (page 12). Why should knowing who you are in Christ give you a desire to grow spiritually? This is a thought-provoking question. Encourage students to think about their answers.
- Give special emphasis to the sections *Where Is Your Meaning?* and *You Are an Ambassador* (pages 13 and 14). Suggested learning activities: Use a circle response and have each student give a brief response to the same question. No one can respond twice until each one has responded. A question you could use: If you are created for good works (Ephesians 2:10), what is one good work you believe God has in store for you? What is an ambassador? List one responsibility of an ambassador. Be creative in writing your own questions. Use questions that will cause students to think and share.

Activities for Application.

- Discuss as a total group or in buzz groups the *Putting It All Together* section.
- Review the *application activities* for the week, and make sure your students begin a list of individuals for whom they want to pray. Pray as a group for these different individuals. Begin to establish a togetherness and joint purpose in seeing different friends come to Christ.

CHAPTER TWO—BUT CAN I DO IT?

Central Truth. A fruitful ministry is a result of Jesus Christ working in us and through us. Our responsibility is to abide in (trust) him and involve ourselves in those things that would build our personal relationship with our Lord.

Purposes. Actually, there are three reasons for this chapter. First, to help our students overcome the fear of ministering to others. Second, to help our students avoid spiritual burnout—the result of looking upon a ministry with a works mind-set, relying just on our own abilities. And third, to address the "I'm not gifted" mentality.

Successful ministry really is a supernatural feat. In God's economy he is the one who brings the results. We are just faithful servants. Our responsibility is to build our love relationship with Jesus Christ and to abide in him. Ministry is not an issue of trying but an issue of trusting. This study helps establish this priority.

Emphasis for Understanding.

- Have your students illustrate their perception of John 15 through a sketch, poetry, a song, a graffiti poster, a collage or montage, a simple design, etc.
- Use the two questions from *A Relational Life Style* (page 20) for buzz group topics. Have the students come back together and share their responses. This helps them begin to zero in on the personal application of this study. If you have time, you could have each student list on the board one word that would describe a healthy relationship with Christ and one word that would describe an unhealthy relationship.
- In pairs have them discuss the personal questions under *Love You? Well . . . uh . . .* (page 23).

Activities for Application.

- From the *Putting It All Together* section (page 24) ask for their personal response to John 15:16.
- Give your students ten to fifteen minutes to think through the personal development worksheet. Use this worksheet for discussion when you have personal appointments with each student.

CHAPTER THREE—YOUR MINISTRY AT HOME

Central Truth. Our relationship to our families is second only to our relationship with Jesus Christ. Therefore, a good ministry begins by first building good relationships within the home.

Purposes. Here is a good rule of thumb. If we do not learn to build good relationships in our homes, it is difficult to build good relationships outside the home—and relationships are the basis of ministry. The purpose of this study is simply to help our learners focus on their priorities at home as they become more involved in Christian service. Many church experts believe the greatest problem in the Body of Christ is the segregation of age groups. While this is necessary in some learning situations, it should be avoided in the home, and this is where we, as leaders, must be committed to the *total* family.

Emphasis for Understanding.

- If you are discussing this study with adults, have them approach the questions in terms of their relationships with their children and spouses. Spend some time creatively going through the study to gear it for adults.
- Have students draw a sketch or symbol that would illustrate their feelings about their homes.

- The last questions and statement in *The Family Plan* (page 27) are excellent for discussion in buzz groups. Have students express opinions. Have them give Scriptures to support their opinions. You could have a panel prepared to discuss this.
- Discuss in pairs the question concerning 1 Peter 2:18-21 and the following application question (page 30).

Activities for Application.

- As a group or in pairs, go through questions in *Some Questions to Think About* (page 31).
- Give time for each student to work through the family needs work sheet. Use this work sheet as a topic of discussion when on personal appointments with your students.
- Be sure each student completes the *action project* and makes his plans. This can simply be a transfer from the family needs work sheet.
- When you meet personally with your disciples, talk about this study and their relationships at home. Discuss their plans to strengthen those relationships. Ask how you can be a servant to them in this area.

CHAPTER FOUR—SOCIALIZING IN SAMARIA

Central Truth. Christ died for each and every individual. His love has no bounds; therefore, we must be available to share his love with all people, both those who may be like us and those who may be different.

Purposes. Whether we realize it or not, most Christians do not have a sensitivity for the unbelievers around them. This study is simply intended to help our students begin to turn their attention away from themselves and refocus on those around them who are not Christians. It will hit home. Gently help your students apply it to their lives.

Emphasis for Understanding.

- Discuss the wrong way and the right way believers should act toward unbelievers. Have students divide into buzz groups, and then come back and share the wealth of their discussions.
- Have students role play an interaction between a Christian and a non-Christian. Have them act out what they think are the common wrong attitudes demonstrated by Christians, and then a right way to relate. You could have students prepare a skit beforehand.
- Excellent discussion questions are in *Wrong Attitudes* (page 35).
- Let several students share their experiences in response to the last two questions in *Getting God's Perspective* (page 37).

Activities for Application.

- Give time for students to work through the "Becoming All Things Work Sheet" (page 38). Have them discuss their plans.
- Discuss the *Putting It All Together* section as a group.
- Discuss the progress of their family application activities from the week before.
- Assign their testimony work project. This is an excellent project to help students think through and verbalize their relationship with Christ. Have one or two students share their testimonies at your next group meeting and continue to do so each week until all have shared.

CHAPTER FIVE—UNCOVERING SPIRITUAL INTEREST

Central Truth. Every person has a spiritual interest and desire to know the One who created him. Our ministry of evangelism begins by allowing God to use us to uncover that spiritual interest.

Purposes. As we study the Scriptures, we see that there is a balance taught in terms of our approach to evangelism. There is friendship involved in evangelism, and there is within that friendship a clear command to take the initiative and share—to be aggressive. In other words, in the Scriptures, we see friendship evangelism and aggressive evangelism. It is not either/or—God uses both ways. I like to call it friendship *in* evangelism.

In this study, we establish the need to take the initiative in uncovering spiritual interest. We want to help our students begin to focus on the spiritual needs of those around them, realize that people are hungry to know God, and to think of creative ways that they can show interest and uncover those needs.

Emphasis for Understanding.

- In *The Friendship Factor* (page 42), use the last question for discussion in pairs. Give students two minutes to come up with two good, creative ideas. Then share the wealth.
- In pairs or buzz groups, have your students discuss answers to the last three questions in *Arousing Spiritual Curiosity* (pages 43 and 44). This is the practical help your students need to get started in their evangelism. We have purposely not provided answers to these questions in order to make you and your students thoroughly think through your approach to creative evangelism.

- Have students role play practical ways to uncover spiritual interest.

Activities for Application.
- Give time for each student to thoroughly think through the friendship work sheets at the end of the chapter. Have students share their plans.
- Review clearly the action activities for the week.

CHAPTER SIX—MAKING THE MESSAGE CLEAR
Central Truth. Sharing Christ means being clear and logical in our communication. Jesus used a progression of four truths as he helped the Samaritan woman understand the good news. We should use these four truths also.

Purpose. The big question most students ask when it comes to evangelism is "What do I say?" In this study we discuss the content of our message. This includes the truth or facts one needs to hear in order to put his faith in Jesus Christ.

There is no question that a great problem in evangelism is clarity. A lot of what people think is evangelism is nothing more than vague generalities, talking in circles, and chasing rabbits down different trails—all dead-end.

We want our students to be clear communicators. We want them to know how to ask people if they want to receive Christ, and how to deal with their response, whether it is "yes," "no," or "I don't know."

This is an important study and requires some good learning activities. Be creative.

Emphasis for Understanding.

- I would recommend that you get hold of some evangelistic tools to help your students understand the logical progression of sharing the gospel. Suggestions: *The Four Spiritual Laws* booklet, *Steps to Peace with God, Four Steps Up,* or another tool of your choice. Explain to your students that tools are designed simply as resources in their communication, and they should be creative in using them. They should not feel that tools "cramp their style." They control the tool, the tool does not control them. Your students will appreciate the use of one of these booklets to help them get started in their evangelism.
- Emphasize *Defining the Problem* (page 51) and *God's Solution* (page 53) by: Having students define sin; have students role play how we can get off the subject in our evangelism and how to avoid the problem. (See last paragraph in *God's Solution*.)
- Use this discussion question in clarifying the section *Making the Solution Clear* (page 53): How can you make sure that people do not get a wrong concept of what it means to be a Christian? How will they get the right concept?
- Review and discuss the Scriptures in each section that help communicate the gospel. Give a quick quiz to help the students recall these Scriptures. Ask them to memorize the references before your next meeting and give another quick quiz then.
- It is very important to have the students role play a witnessing experience, either by using a tool or by using their Bibles. Have them practice sharing the gospel with each other. Allow enough time in your session for this practice. Have them practice responding to a "yes" response and to a "no" response. Ask them to decide what they would do if someone

responded, "I don't know whether I want to receive Christ."

- Be sure to thoroughly discuss *Answering Questions* (page 57).

Activities for Application.

- Give a quick quiz on the four specific truths Jesus used to communicate the gospel in John 4.

  1. The positive approach: God's positive love and plan for man (verse 10).
  2. Defining the problem: Sin separates us from God (verses 16-18).
  3. God's solution: Christ died for our sins (verse 25).
  4. Our response: We must personally receive Christ (verse 26).

- In buzz groups have them discuss the questions in the *Putting It All Together* section.
- Have your students decide on the people they want to share Christ with this week. Pray together as a group for the people they want to share with. Help your students focus on the needs of their non-Christian friends, rather than on their own fears.

CHAPTER SEVEN—TAKING THE INITIATIVE

Central Truth. If we are going to be used of God to meet needs and introduce individuals to Christ, we must:

. . . take the initiative.
. . . relax in the Spirit.
. . . be clear in our communication.
. . . not argue with those with whom we share.

Purpose. It is often the little things that make a difference, isn't it? When it comes to communicating Jesus

Christ, we want our students to succeed and have good experiences. In this study, we discuss some of the little things, such as attitudes and actions, that will help them as they share God's love with others. We also talk about our responsibility in taking the initiative to share Christ—the biggest obstacle every Christian must overcome. Jesus said to "go." Let's help our students go. In fact, let's set the pace.

Emphasis for Understanding.

- Have your students discuss their idea of being casual but definite in their witness. Have them role play their idea of this concept. (See *Being Casual but Definite,* page 61.)
- Discuss in detail (pairs or buzz groups) how to freshly communicate different terms listed in *Clear Communication.* Discuss why Christian lingo does not communicate and how a non-Christian might perceive this lingo.
- Have students prepare a skit on a wrong way to witness and a right way to witness. It can be humorous.
- Here are some suggestions to emphasize the truths in *Reacting or Responding* (page 62): Have your students list several difficult circumstances they could possibly run into when sharing their faith, and then have them role play how they would react to these circumstances; in pairs, have them create a cartoon strip that depicts a humorous look at reacting and responding when witnessing.
- Have students study Acts 17:16-34 in buzz groups, and list principles for evangelism. Come together, and share the wealth.
- Discuss innovative ways to create opportunities to share Christ (point five in *Attitudes for Taking the Initiative,* page 64).

- If they so desire, have your students team up as prayer partners and witnessing partners as suggested in the chapter.

Activities for Application.
- Have each student complete the statement, "The most significant thing I have learned in this study is . . . ."
- From the section entitled *My Action This Week,* have each student complete the work sheet and share his plans for creative opportunities to share Christ.

CHAPTER EIGHT—SERVING YOUNG CHRISTIANS

Central Truth. Young believers in Christ need a servant to help them get a proper start in their walk with Christ and guide them along the way. We begin serving young believers by building relationships.

Purposes. Up to this point in our book, we have discussed leading people to Christ. Now we begin a series of three studies giving insight and direction for helping Christians grow.

In evangelism, relationships are important. But in discipleship they are absolutely essential. This essential is perhaps summed up best in Paul's words from 1 Thessalonians 2:7, 8: "But we proved to be gentle among you, as a nursing mother tenderly cares for her own children. Having thus a fond affection for you, we were well pleased to impart to you not only the gospel but also our own lives, because you have become very dear to us" (NASB).

In this study we want to help our students focus on the importance of being a servant and a friend to young Christians.

Emphasis for Understanding.

- From *Being a Servant* (page 68), have each student share one need he thinks is critical in a new Christian's life. List these needs on the board or overhead projector. No need can be listed twice. This forces your students to think.
- From *Two Ways to Lead* (page 69), have students role play their concept of two types of leaders. Or have several students come prepared with a skit to illustrate the leadership styles. Have students discuss the pros and the cons of both styles.
- Suggestions to help with the understanding of 1 Peter 5:2-5: In pairs or buzz groups have students discuss and answer the questions in *Attitudes of a Servant* (page 69); have students write a short paraphrase of verses 2 through 5.

Activities for Application.

- In buzz groups, have students list practical ways to serve young Christians. Come back together, and share the wealth.
- In the *Putting It All Together* section (page 73), have students discuss responses to questions.
- In pairs or as a total group, have students work through the action assignment for the week.

CHAPTER NINE—BUILDING YOUNG CHRISTIANS

Central Truth. Our responsibility to young Christians includes being a teacher—someone who knows what young Christians need to learn and is willing to teach them.

Purposes. Teaching God's Word is perhaps the aspect of discipleship we all identify with most. The disciple is a learner, and a learner needs a teacher.

In this study we take this whole responsibility of teaching young Christians and put it into a very practical framework. We ask questions that make our students think—questions that build a foundation of motivation and direction for accomplishing the job.

First, we answer the question, "What does a new Christian need to learn?" Then, "How can we help him learn these things?" This is the beginning of what we call *relational thinking.* For a closer look at the principles of relational thinking and terminal thinking, see *A Guidebook to Discipleship* by Hartman and Sutherland (Harvest House Publishers, Portland, Oregon).

Emphasis for Understanding.

- This study has loads of learning projects already included. Use the projects to their maximum.
- Have students, working in pairs, develop their own illustrations on relational thinking and terminal thinking. Encourage them to use illustrations from their own lives. Help them to see that a great deal of our activity really is terminal activity.
- In buzz groups or pairs, thoroughly discuss the questions in *Learning to Be Relational* (page 79). These are the key questions of the entire study. Most of us do not have a clear handle on why we do what we do in our ministries. These questions help get our students off to the right start in their personal ministries. This is the heart of motivation—helping people understand why they do what they do.
- Bring a copy of *So You Want Solutions* to your meeting, and introduce the book to your students. Make copies available to them for the people they are following up.

Activities for Application.

- Discuss the *Putting It All Together* section—good interaction questions.

- Discuss and review the *Let's Get Started* section (page 82). Field questions they may have.
- Have students discuss their experiences in building relationships with their young disciples during the week before. Have a question and answer time to discuss any difficulties.
- Be available to your students during the week to answer questions and give direction in their follow-up ministries. If you cannot meet with them personally, telephone them.

CHAPTER TEN—DARE TO MULTIPLY

Central Truth. Spiritual multiplication is God's plan for reaching the world and fulfilling the Great Commission. We can be confident that God wants us to involve ourselves in multiplication—training faithful men and women who will be equipped to pass his truth on to others.

Purposes. Helping our students develop a vision and a sense of destiny is one of the greatest ministries we can have in their lives. In *Dare to Multiply,* we want to give a challenge to dig into personal ministry in its purest form—spiritual multiplication. There is no higher calling in all of life. Give this study your best shot!

Emphasis for Understanding.

- To help your students begin to gain a vision for the world, here are some suggestions:

  Bring to your group statistics of population in your city, country, even the world.

  Discuss the need in your own city and even in your own community.

  Discuss how a ministry of multiplication could have a tremendous impact in your city.

Bring some missionary reports on the great needs around the world.

- Have students draw a picture or symbol that would illustrate 2 Timothy 2:2.
- In pairs have students design a simple poster or brochure that would be an advertisement for a multiplication ministry.
- For three minutes, and in pairs, have them discuss their responses to the questions in *Are You Learning* (page 90)?
- In pairs or buzz groups discuss the questions in *Developing Leaders* and *Selecting Potential Multipliers* (pages 93 and 94). Come together, and share the wealth.

Activities for Application.

- Discuss the questions in *Putting It All Together* (page 95).
- Have as many students as possible share their responses to the last two questions of the section. Emphasize the question on life objectives.
- Meet with each student personally within the next two weeks, and discuss together his plans for a personal multiplication ministry. Many of your students will be involved in a ministry to new Christians, so you will want to continue to lead them and monitor what they are doing.

Challenge your students to a new group where you can continue to sharpen your ministry skills and grow together in your relationship with Christ. Review the books suggested at the back of the chapter as possible guidebooks for your discussions (page 96).